THIS BOOK BELONGS TO

IVY BB POK

Once upon a time,
somewhere in a jungle
far away

in a farting family,
a monkey named Tom
was born.

Tom loved to eat
unripe green bananas,
and he farted even more.

He loved fooling around
and had a good time.

He learned from
his older sister

and he enjoyed
going to school,

in which even
the teacher farted
stinky farts.

Thanks to his farts,

Tom was the fastest monkey in the whole jungle.

SCHOOL

Once, on his way,
he met a baby elephant
in trouble.

The elephant
fell into a deep hole.

Tom quickly
had a brilliant idea

and decided to feed
the baby elephant
with green bananas.

After eating them,

little Lisa let out
a huge fart that lifted her
into the air.

Tom decided to
escort his new friend home

and they farted all the way.

The elephant joyfully fell into the arms of her mother,

who, out of happiness,
let out a stinky fart too.

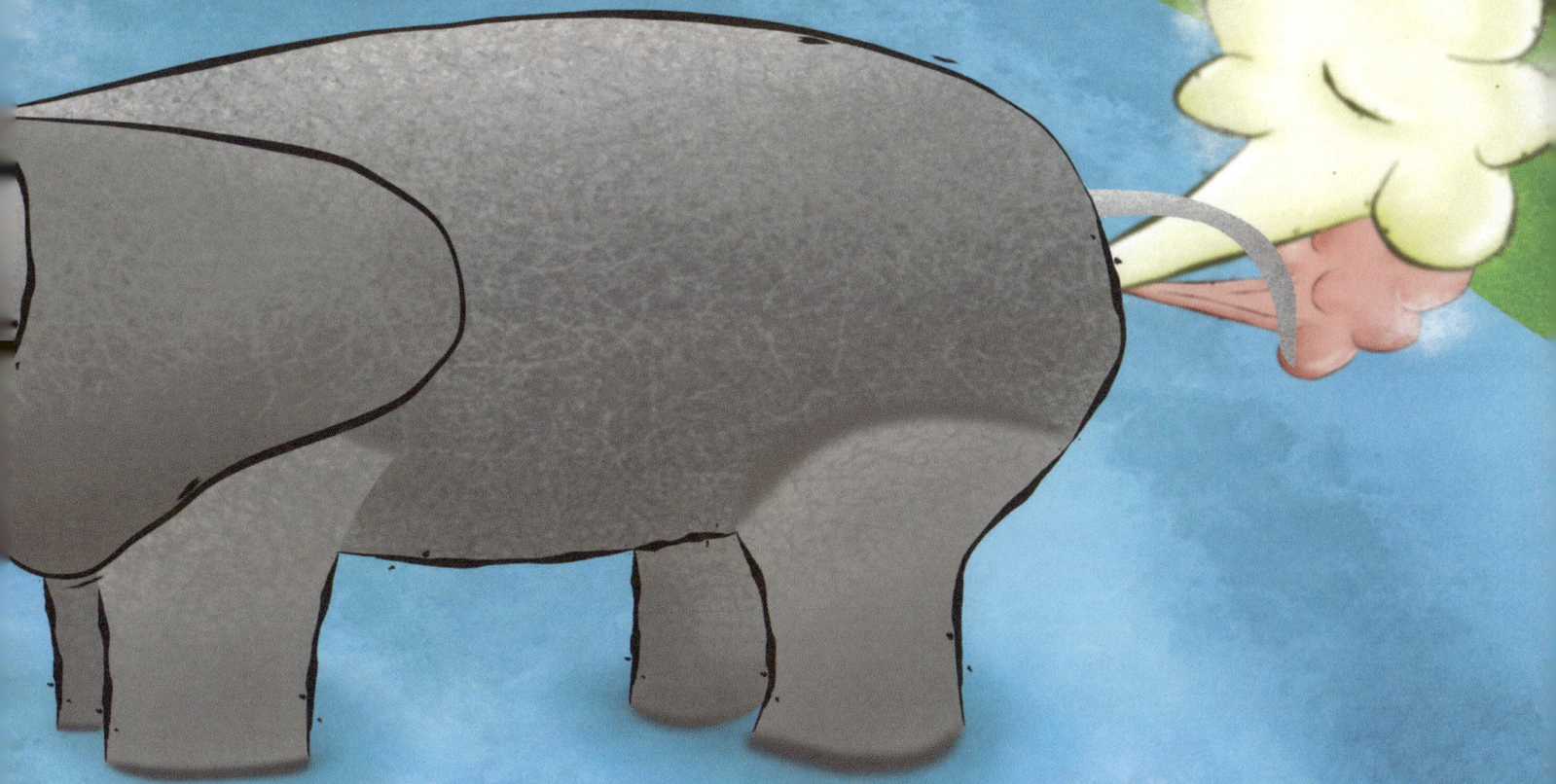

Tom quietly returned home eating his favorite green bananas on the way,

where in the evening,
by the fire,
he told his family

about his adventure and
a new friend,
an elephant named Lisa.

This is not the end
of Tom's farting adventures.
Soon I will tell you
about his next adventure.

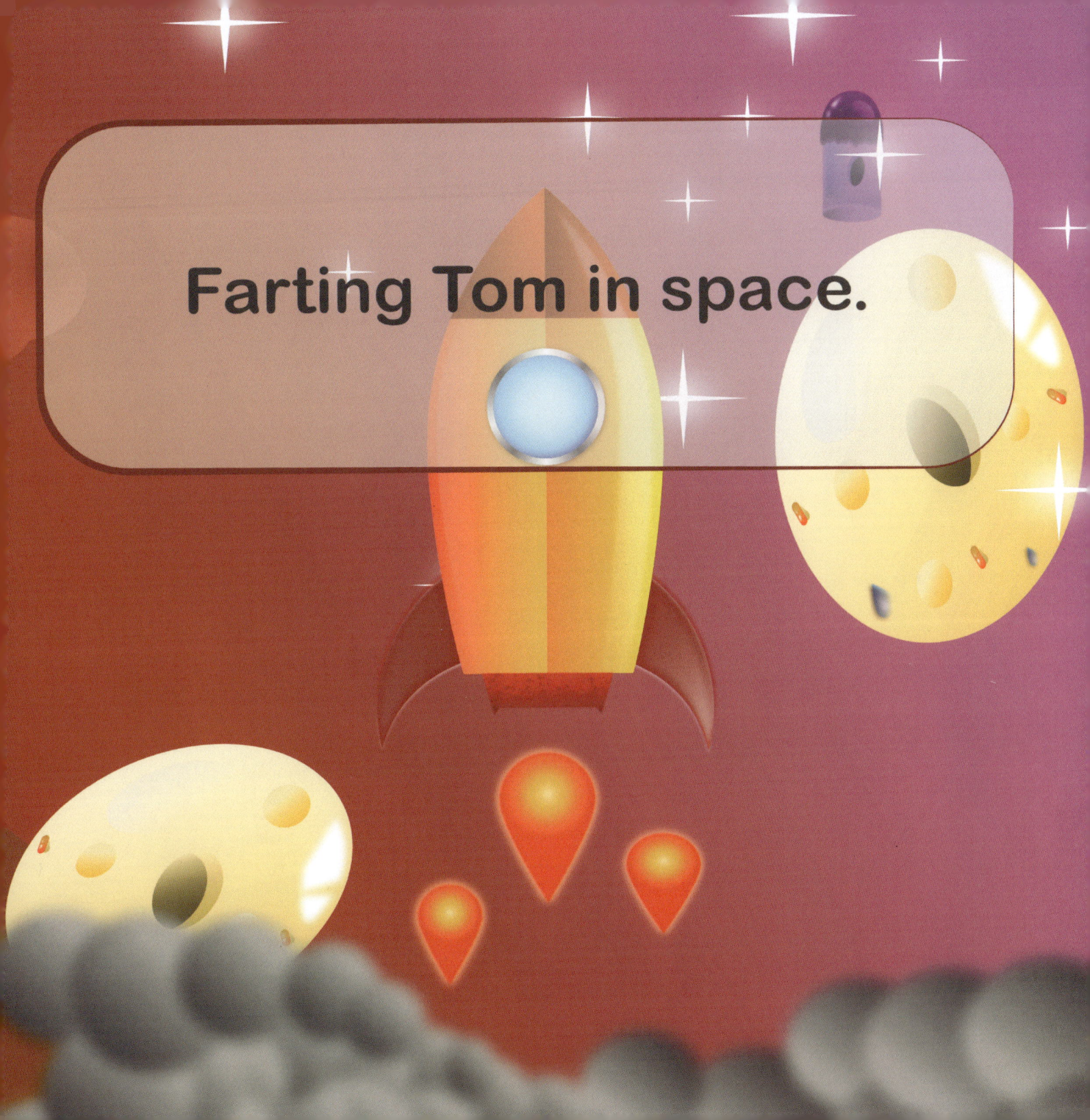

Farting Tom in space.

Printed in Great Britain
by Amazon